TO:
FROM:

DINNER WITH THE KING

HOW KING DAVID'S INVITATION SHOWS US GOD'S LOVE

Written by
PAUL TAUTGES

Illustrated by
INGRID SAWUBONA

It's exciting to be invited to a friend's house, isn't it?
We immediately start wondering ...

What will our friend's house look like?
Do they have a big backyard?
What kinds of food will we eat?
Will there be lots of other kids?
Will there be cake?

BUT . . .

What if a
king invited you
to his palace?
THAT WOULD REALLY BE
THE BEST INVITATION
EVER!
JUST
IMAGINE . . .
You are
invited

Amazing playgrounds!
Huge towers!
Scrumptious food!
And lots of fun people to meet!
But do you know the best part of the invitation?
TO BE WITH THE KING HIMSELF!
Let me tell you how I know …

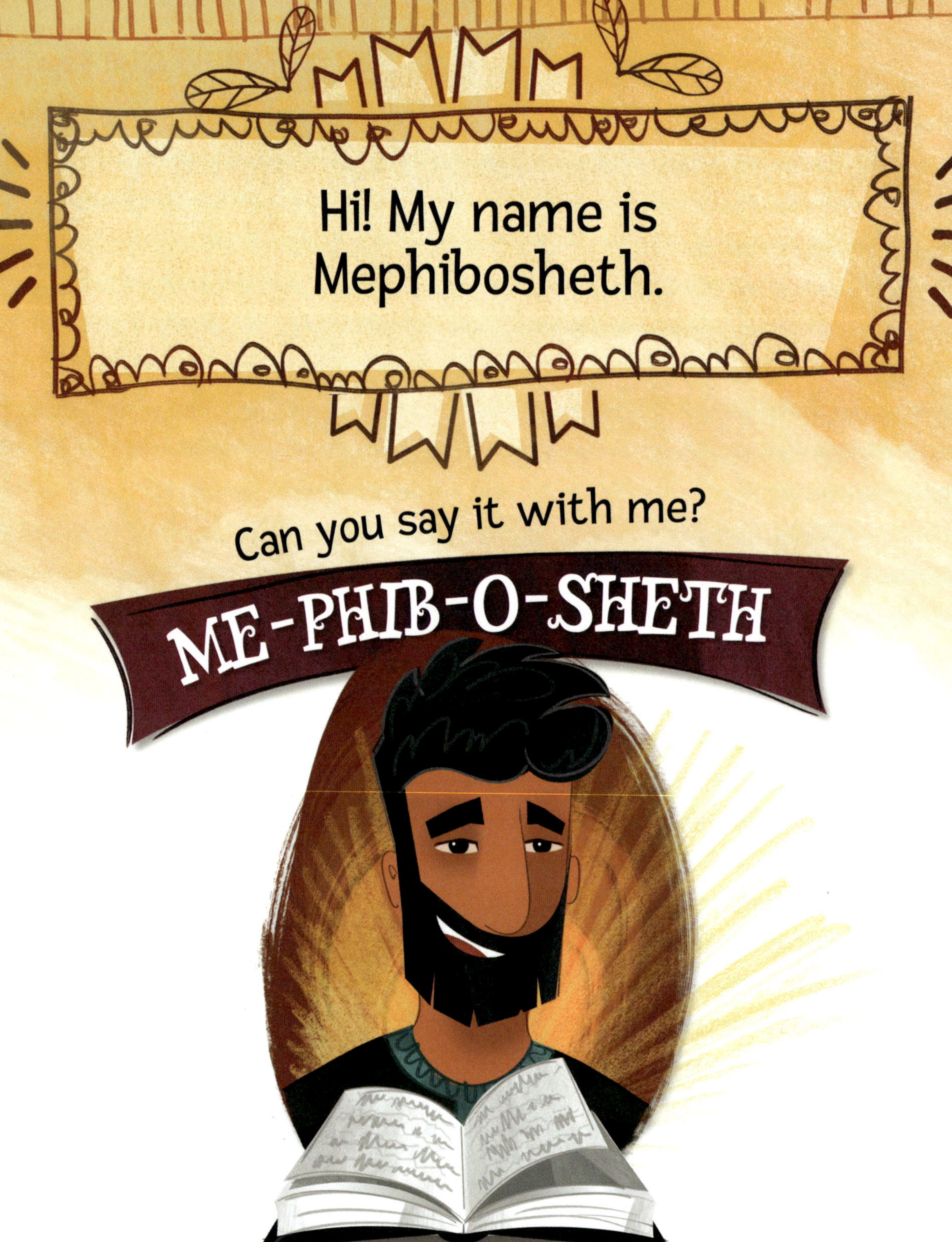

You can read my story in God's Book, the holy Bible.*

*(2 Samuel 9)

My grandpa was the king of Israel, and my dad was a prince.

But when I was just five years old, there was a terrible war in the land.

Many people died, including my dad and my grandpa.

So when the bad news reached our house, everyone, including my babysitter, panicked and ran away as fast as they could.

But she dropped me, and I broke both of my feet.

My feet were broken so badly that I could never walk again.
I couldn't go **ANYWHERE** by myself.

Someone had to carry me everywhere I needed to go.

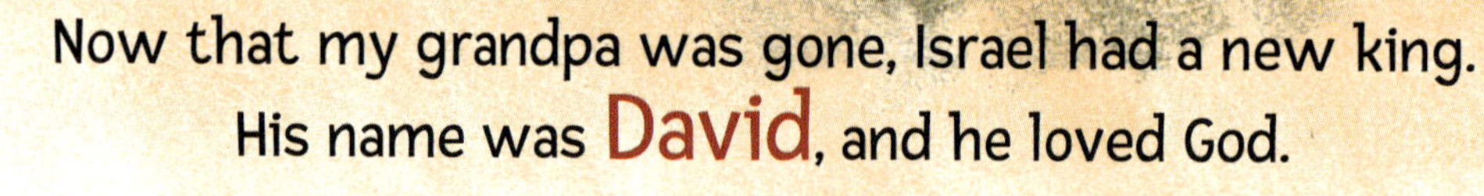

Now that my grandpa was gone, Israel had a new king.
His name was **David**, and he loved God.

He was a shepherd and a powerful warrior, and the people of Israel loved him because he protected them just like he protected his sheep.

THAT SOUNDS LIKE GOOD NEWS, RIGHT?

The problem is this: my grandpa and King David were BIG enemies. My grandpa even tried to kill him a few times!

But one day, years later, I got a royal invitation.
King David wanted me to come to his palace.

Oh no! I was sure I was in BIG trouble.
Because of my grandpa, I was King David's enemy! Maybe he would KILL me!

I wished I could run away,
but I knew I had to go.
My friends carried me
into the palace where
King David was waiting.

He looked at me ...

AND HE SMILED!

WELCOME!
he said.
COME IN AND HAVE DINNER WITH ME.

I was so scared that I said
what I was thinking right out loud!
WHY ARE YOU BEING SO KIND TO ME?
MY GRANDPA TRIED TO KILL YOU!

HE DID,
King David said.
But did you know your dad was my best friend? When God chose me to be the next king, your grandpa was very angry. But your dad was kind to me.
I'VE BEEN LOOKING FOR YOU BECAUSE ...

I DON'T JUST WANT YOU TO EAT WITH ME TODAY ...
I want you to stay at my palace with me and ALWAYS eat at my table, just like one of my own kids.

It didn't matter that I was an enemy of the king! It didn't even matter that I couldn't walk! All that mattered was that King David wanted to make me a part of his family! He truly showed me a lot of grace, don't you think?

But ... what is grace?
GRACE MEANS RECEIVING A GIFT FROM SOMEONE THAT YOU COULD NEVER BE GOOD ENOUGH TO DESERVE OR PAY BACK.
GRACE
I NEEDED GRACE FROM A KING,
AND SO DO YOU!

But not from just any king—

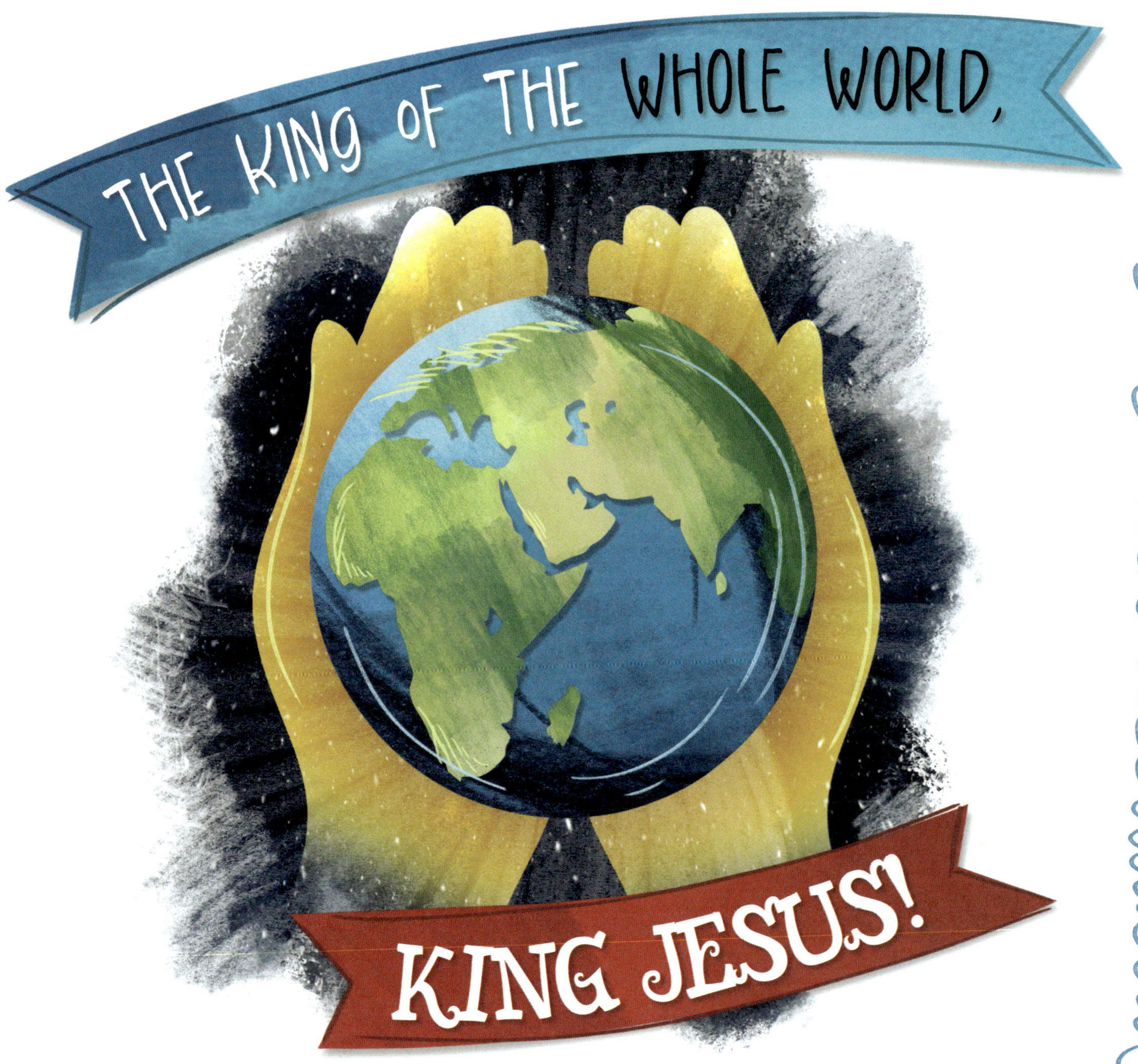

But why do we need grace?

WE NEED GRACE

BECAUSE WE ARE ALL SINNERS WHO DO BAD THINGS.

And sinners are God's enemies who deserve to be punished!

The same Bible that tells you about my story of receiving grace from King David tells the GREATEST STORY OF ALL. It tells how you, too, can receive grace from the King of Heaven.

Jesus, the Son of God, left his throne in heaven.

He came to be with us so we could go to be with him.

God gave his one and only Son to die in your place—for your sin. Even though he did NOTHING wrong, Jesus let his enemies nail him to a cross.

AND THEN GOD DID SOMETHING INCREDIBLE!
He raised Jesus from the dead,
and Jesus went back to heaven.

Living in the palace
was amazing!
I HAD LOTS OF PEOPLE TO HELP ME!

I LIVED IN SPLENDOR!
I HAD A FAMILY AGAIN!
BUT . . .

LIVING IN HEAVEN WILL BE EVEN MORE
WONDERFUL!
NO MORE SICKNESS OR ACCIDENTS!

EVERYTHING WILL BE PERFECT,
AND NOTHING WILL GO WRONG!
WE'LL BELONG TO THE BEST FAMILY EVER—
MADE UP OF PEOPLE FROM EVERY
NATION ON THE EARTH!
AND . . .
do you know the best part of all?

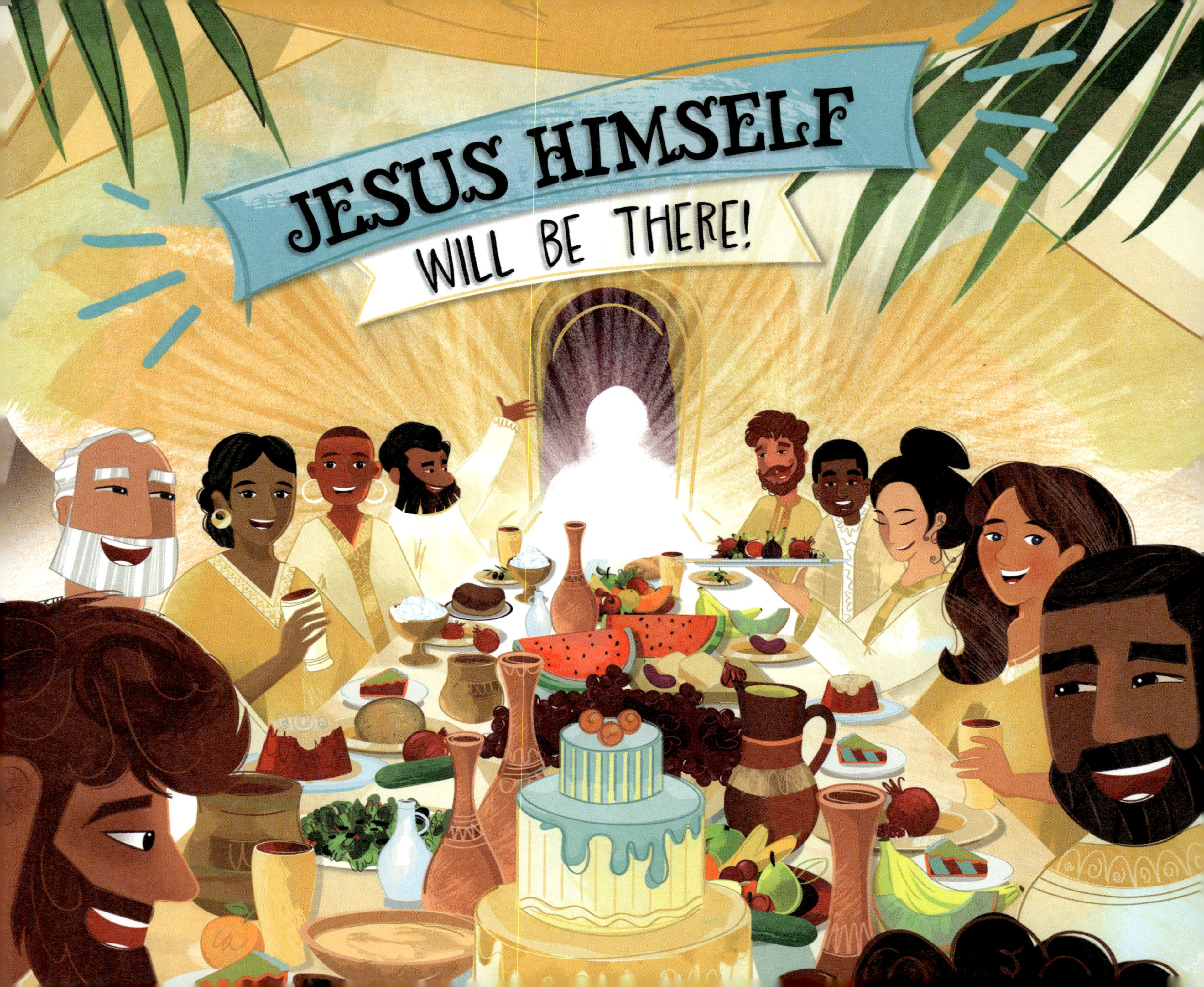
JESUS HIMSELF
WILL BE THERE!

King Jesus is inviting you to come and be with him and be part of his family, FOREVER.

WHAT WILL YOU SAY TO THE KING'S INVITATION?

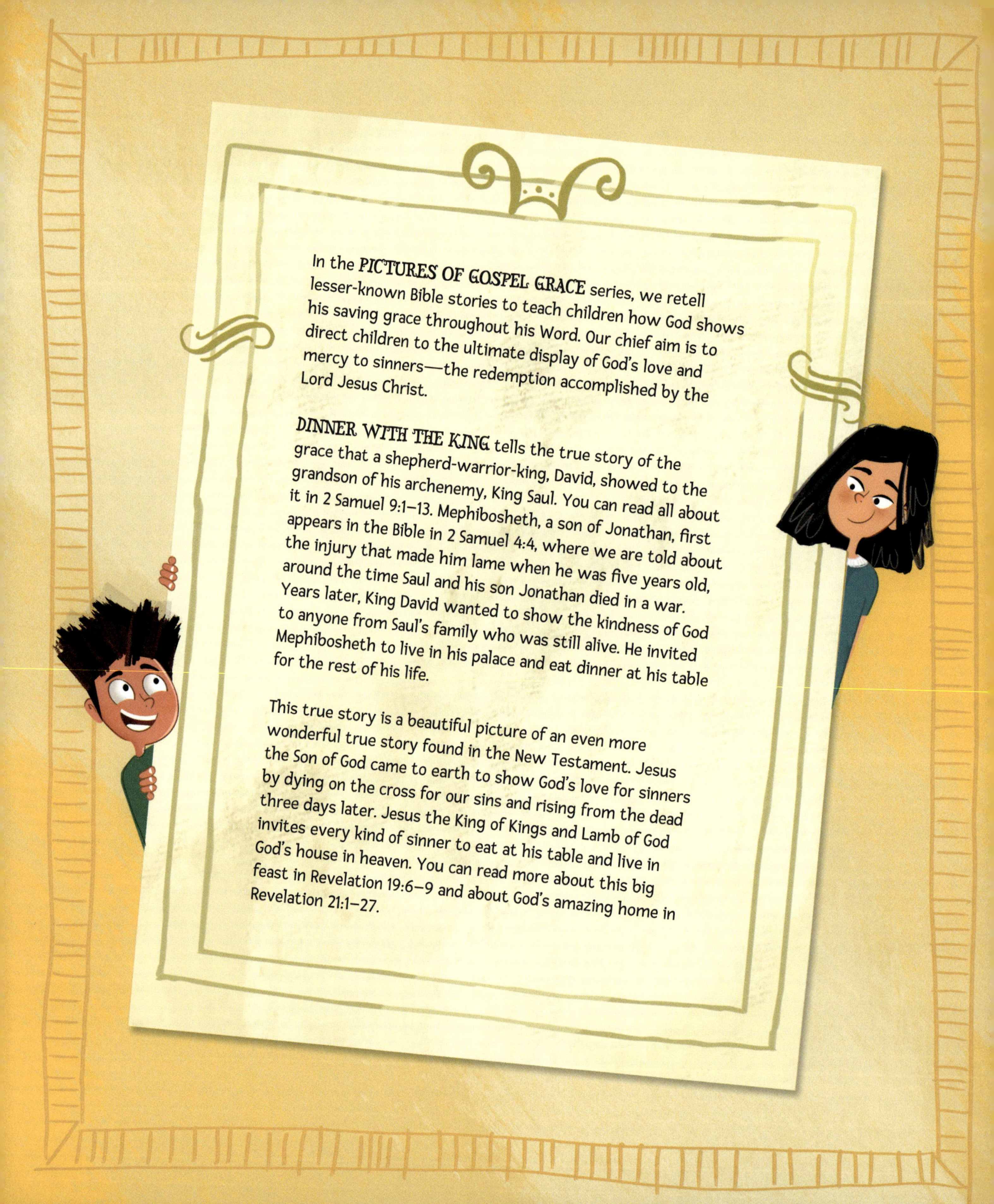

In the **PICTURES OF GOSPEL GRACE** series, we retell lesser-known Bible stories to teach children how God shows his saving grace throughout his Word. Our chief aim is to direct children to the ultimate display of God's love and mercy to sinners—the redemption accomplished by the Lord Jesus Christ.

DINNER WITH THE KING tells the true story of the grace that a shepherd-warrior-king, David, showed to the grandson of his archenemy, King Saul. You can read all about it in 2 Samuel 9:1–13. Mephibosheth, a son of Jonathan, first appears in the Bible in 2 Samuel 4:4, where we are told about the injury that made him lame when he was five years old, around the time Saul and his son Jonathan died in a war. Years later, King David wanted to show the kindness of God to anyone from Saul's family who was still alive. He invited Mephibosheth to live in his palace and eat dinner at his table for the rest of his life.

This true story is a beautiful picture of an even more wonderful true story found in the New Testament. Jesus the Son of God came to earth to show God's love for sinners by dying on the cross for our sins and rising from the dead three days later. Jesus the King of Kings and Lamb of God invites every kind of sinner to eat at his table and live in God's house in heaven. You can read more about this big feast in Revelation 19:6–9 and about God's amazing home in Revelation 21:1–27.

FOR PARENTS, GRANDPARENTS, AND TEACHERS

Below is a glossary of some key words along with simple definitions that will help to guide your discussion of this book. We encourage you to look up the Scripture passages and read them with the children in your life.

BIBLE. God's Book, his holy Word, given to show us what God is like and to tell us how we can become his children and friends when we trust in Jesus Christ. The Bible always tells us the truth. *Read John 5:24.*

ENEMY. Someone who hates you and wants to stay far away from you. The **Bible** says we are all enemies of God because we turn away from him to do whatever we want. The good news is that Jesus took our **punishment** so that enemies like us could turn into his friends. *Read Isaiah 53:6; 1 Peter 2:24.*

FOREVER. Time that never runs out. We are always running out of time, so this is hard to understand. The **Bible** says God has always existed forever (not like us, who had to be born), and when we **repent** and trust in Jesus, we will someday live with him forever. *Read Revelation 22:1–5.*

GRACE. A gift we receive that we could never be good enough to deserve or pay back. Because we naturally want to disobey God and stay away from him, we can never become his friends on our own. But God, who loves to show kindness to us, did what we could never do for ourselves: Jesus took the **punishment** for all we have done wrong and gives us new hearts that trust in him. *Read 2 Corinthians 5:21; Ephesians 2:8–10.*

INVITATION. When someone asks you to come to their house. Like Mephibosheth, we don't deserve to be invited to the King's palace. Yet the **Bible** tells us that the Lord Jesus Christ invites **sinners** like us to **repent**, become his friends, and live with him **forever**. *Read Matthew 11:28–30.*

PUNISH. To make someone pay for what they did wrong. We deserve to be punished with death for disobeying God, but Jesus Christ chose to be punished by God in our place. Because Jesus died for us, God forgives us and makes us live **forever** when we **repent** and trust in him. *Read 1 Peter 3:18.*

REPENT. To turn around and go the other direction, away from doing whatever we want and toward God and his love. God's gift of **grace** helps us to understand we are his **enemies** and changes our hearts so that we don't want to disobey God anymore but instead trust in Jesus as our Savior, King, and Friend. *Read Luke 5:27–32; 2 Peter 3:9.*

SINNER. Someone who does not love God or do what he tells them to do because they love themselves and their own way more. The **Bible** teaches that every one of us is a sinner. We are all selfish and disobey God, and we all deserve to be **punished**. *Read Romans 3:23–25; 6:23.*

Mephibosheth had a young son when he moved to David's house!

CAN YOU FIND HIS WIFE AND SON IN THIS BOOK?

Printed in the United States of America

Library of Congress Cataloging-in-Publication Data

Names: Tautges, Paul, author. | Sawubona, Ingrid, 1970- illustrator.
Title: Dinner with the King : how King David's invitation shows us God's love / written by Paul Tautges ; illustrated by Ingrid Sawubona.
Description: Phillipsburg, New Jersey : P&R Publishing Company, [2024] | Audience: Ages 5-9 | Summary: "A scary invitation turns out to be very good news in this playfully illustrated, deeply biblical book for kids ages 5-9. Discover how David's grace to Mephibosheth points to our gospel hope"-- Provided by publisher.
Identifiers: LCCN 2023057114 | ISBN 9781629959986 (hardcover) | ISBN 9781629959993 (epub)
Subjects: LCSH: David, King of Israel--Juvenile literature. | Bible. Old Testament--Juvenile literature.
Classification: LCC BS580.D3 T287 2024 | DDC 222/.4092--dc23/eng/20240212
LC record available at https://lccn.loc.gov/2023057114